SAGA of the ST. LOUIS BLUES

SAGA of the ST. LOUIS BLUES

by Stan Fischler

Photography by
Lew Portnoy / Bob Kolbrener

A Stuart L. Daniels Book

PRENTICE-HALL, INC.
Englewood Cliffs, New Jersey

SAGA OF THE ST. LOUIS BLUES
by Stan Fischler

Copyright © 1972 by The Stuart L. Daniels
Company, Inc.

Published by
Prentice-Hall, Inc.
Englewood Cliffs, New Jersey

Printed in the United States of America • T
Prentice-Hall International, Inc., London
Prentice-Hall of Australia, Pty. Ltd., Sydney
Prentice-Hall of Canada, Ltd., Toronto
Prentice-Hall of India Private Ltd., New Delhi
Prentice-Hall of Japan, Inc., Tokyo

Library of Congress Catalog Card Number: 72-7614
ISBN: 0-13-785931-7 (paperbound)

ISBN: 0-13-785923-6 (hardbound)

Dedication

To a terrific inspirational line up—
Shirley, Benjamin, Molly, Joetta,
Chuck, Chazy, Sybil, and Max.

Acknowledgments

The author wishes to thank Michael Rubin,
Nancy Demmon, and Amy Newman, who helped
so much in the preparation of this book.

The St. Louis Arena. Full-house.

when hockey was young

Newcomers to the St. Louis ice hockey scene may not realize that the local popularity of the game reaches back into the Roaring Twenties, when hockey was played in the city's old Winter Garden. However, the great leap forward, ice-wise, took place in 1929 when the St. Louis Arena was completed, a modernistic structure decades ahead of its time both in appearance and in structural design.

The Arena's vaulted roof, originally made of wood, utilized the same engineering principles as the renowned Houston Astrodome built more than three decades later. The dome of the Arena rises majestically 135 feet above the floor, and a program of growth has added room for more than 18,000 to its ice hockey seating capacity.

The First Pro Team

Although the Arena had a roof, seats, and a box office, it lacked ice until 1932. That year the city's first professional hockey team, the Flyers, which had its debut in 1928 in the American Hockey Association, became tenants of the Arena.

The Flyers dispatched many aces to the National Hockey League. Not the least of them was Lynn Patrick, today the St. Louis Blues vice-president, who graduated to the NHL's New York Rangers in 1934–35. It was during that time that St. Louis enjoyed its first taste of major league hockey.

Early in the Autumn of 1934 the Board of Governors of the National Hockey League learned that the Ottawa Senators hockey club was having serious problems and could not continue operations in Canada's capital city. Directors of the Ottawa club received permission to switch the franchise to St. Louis, where fresh financing was available. The club was renamed the Eagles.

This move collided head-on with the Flyers of the American Association, who challenged the NHL's right to invade their domain. After threatening a damage suit against the Eagles, the Flyers simmered down, and the newest NHL club opened at the Arena on November 8, 1934, losing 3–1 to the Chicago Black Hawks. A crowd of 12,600 was recorded for the opener, which featured a ceremonial face-off by Mayor Bernard Dickman.

The St. Louis Eagles

Just two nights later the St. Louis sextet won its first NHL game, defeating the New York Rangers 4–2. Of particular interest to the new fans was the fact that Lynn Patrick made his NHL debut that night, playing left wing on a Ranger line with Bert Connolly and Charlie Mason.

Joy as to the future of the team was short-lived. The Eagles lost their next eight consecutive games. They did not win their second match of the 1934–35 NHL season until December 4, 1934, when goalie Bill Beveridge shut out the New York Americans 2–0 at the Arena. But

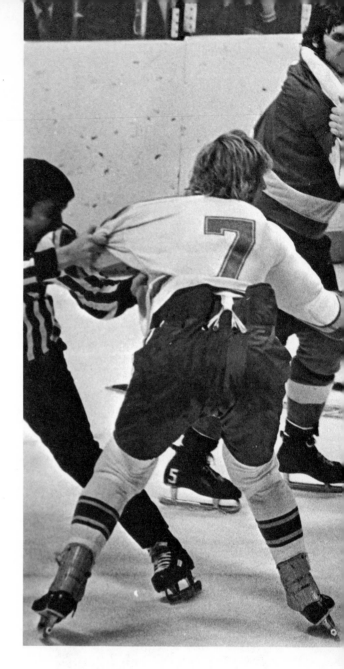

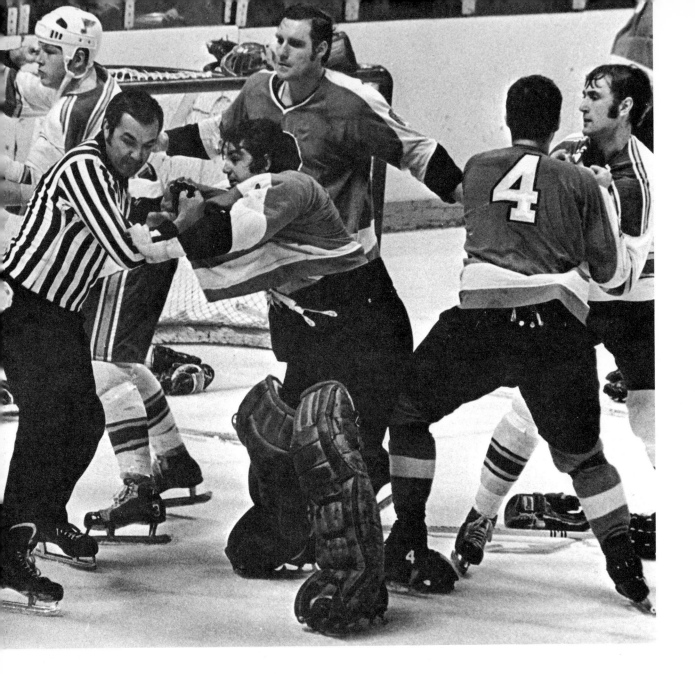

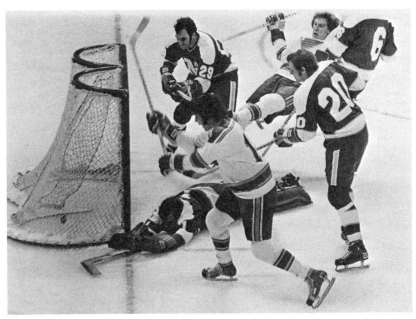

Phil Roberto shoots and scores against Minnesota's Gump Worsley. Dean Prentice (29) and Tom Reid (20) find it hard to believe.

Sometimes the other team scores.

the Eagles couldn't put two victories back-to-back and were beaten 1–0 by the Montreal Maroons in their next game.

After 13 matches, St. Louis only had two wins to show. As it inevitably does in these cases, the axe fell on manager Eddie Gerard, who was replaced by George Boucher, an outstanding NHL defenseman who had ended his playing days with the Chicago Black Hawks. However, the Eagles fortunes changed little, and at mid-season St. Louis was resting on the bottom of the Canadian Division of the NHL—the Montreal Canadiens, New York Americans, Montreal Maroons, and Toronto Maple Leafs were the other teams in the division—with a record of five wins, three ties, and sixteen losses.

Under the circumstances, it was hardly surprising that home attendance was undergoing a steady decline. Suggestions were even made that some home games be transferred back to Ottawa, where the strong interest in hockey might net a larger attendance. Managing director Clare Brunton rejected that idea, but the St. Louis management betrayed its fears of collapse by executing a series of deals which later turned out to be disastrous to the Eagles.

At the time, St. Louis boasted one especially potent forward line comprised of Syd Howe—no relation to Gordie—on left wing, Frank Finnegan on right wing, and Bill Cowley at center. Howe was among the league-leading scorers; Cowley was a young potential superstar; and Finnegan was a reliable veteran.

When the attendance panic set in, the Eagles management peddled Howe to Detroit for cash; he eventually played so expertly that he was inducted into the Hockey Hall of Fame. Finnegan was sold to Toronto. Another player, Ralph Bowman, was sold to Detroit.

Downfall of the Eagles

The Eagles played their final game of the season in St. Louis on March 12, 1935, defeating Detroit 3–2. Rather appropriately, they closed out the disastrous season at Maple Leaf Gardens in Toronto, losing 5–3. The final tabulation showed eleven victories, six ties and thirty-one defeats for the Eagles, the worst record in the NHL.

Although rumors abounded that St. Louis would lose its NHL team, the Eagles' fate was not sealed until September 28, 1935, when the club requested permission from the NHL Board of Governors to suspend operations for one year. Disapproving the idea, the board suggested that the league option the rights to St. Louis players with the understanding that if the franchise was sold by the league, the purchase price would be paid to St. Louis.

On October 15, 1935, the league agreed to buy the St. Louis players and the franchise. A draft of St. Louis-owned players was held after the governors assigned a cash value to each skater. The lowest-placed teams chose first, with the following results:

First Draft: Peter Kelly, New York Americans, $2,000; Bill Beveridge, Montreal Canadiens, $4,000; Carl Voss, Detroit Red Wings, $4,000; Glen Brydson, New York Rangers, $4,000; Joe Lamb, Montreal Maroons, $3,250; Bill Cowley, Boston Bruins, $2,250; Gerald Shannon, Toronto Maple Leafs, $500.

Second Draft: Eddie Finnegan, New York Americans, $1,250; Irvine Frew, Montreal Canadiens, $2,750; M. Peterkin, Detroit Red Wings, $500; Vernon Ayres, New York Rangers, $2,000; W. Taugher, Montreal Maroons, $2,500; Ted Graham, Boston Bruins, $2,000; Clifford Purpur, Toronto Maple Leafs, $750.

The prize catch, as things turned out, was Cowley, who became the Bruins crack center and an eventual member of the Hockey Hall of Fame. Voss, after a long player career, wound up as referee-in-chief of the NHL, and Purpur later became a Chicago Black Hawks star. Curiously, the Windy City club made no picks in the draft.

Still a Good Hockey Town

Depressing as it was, the demise of the Eagles did not signal the death of hockey in St. Louis. Quite the contrary. After a shaky start, the Flyers developed into an American Hockey Association juggernaut, with an enthusiastic and faithful local following.

Glenn Hall defending against J.P. Parise of Minnesota.

Glenn Hall, no longer with the team, was so good at goaltending that many people suspected that he invented the job. That's why when they came to give him a nick-name it could only be "Mister Goalie!"

St. Louis, which had entered the AHA in 1928–29, finished last for its first three seasons. By 1931–32 the Flyers had climbed to fourth place in the six-team league, which included Chicago, Kansas City, Duluth, Tulsa, and Buffalo. A year later St. Louis ended second and did the same in 1933–34.

While the NHL Eagles were floundering in their league during the 1934–35, campaign the AHA Flyers finished on top and defeated Kansas City in the playoffs. St. Louis then took on the St. Paul Saints, champions of the old Central Hockey League, and unfortunately were wiped out in three straight games by the Minnesota club.

St. Paul joined the AHA for the 1935–36 season and finished first, 12 points ahead of runner-up St. Louis, but this time the Flyers obtained sweet revenge. They defeated Tulsa in a playoff semifinal and then beat St. Paul three games to two in the AHA finals. By now St. Louis had become the kingpin of the AHA. The Flyers finished first in the 1936–37 season, a whopping 18 points ahead of runner-up Minneapolis. In the playoffs they routed Kansas City in three straight games of the semifinals but were upset by Minneapolis three games to none in the finals.

Cup Winners

That defeat was rectified in 1937–38, when St. Louis not only finished first but knocked off Minneapolis three games to none, in the finals. The victory gained the Flyers the honor of being the first team to have its name engraved on the Harry F. Sinclair Cup, donated by the oil magnate to the AHA.

In 1938–39 St. Louis finished first and once again annexed the Sinclair Trophy. The Flyers led the league again the following year, only to be eliminated in the playoffs.

While this was going on, professional hockey was growing across the United States. The game was progressing from a shoestring operation to major status as fans added ice hockey to their sports interests.

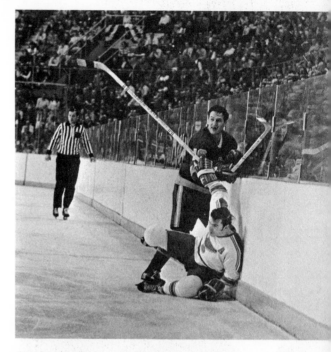

Barclay Plager hits the ice but effectively blocks Bill Lesuk of Los Angeles.

Gerry Odrowski.

14

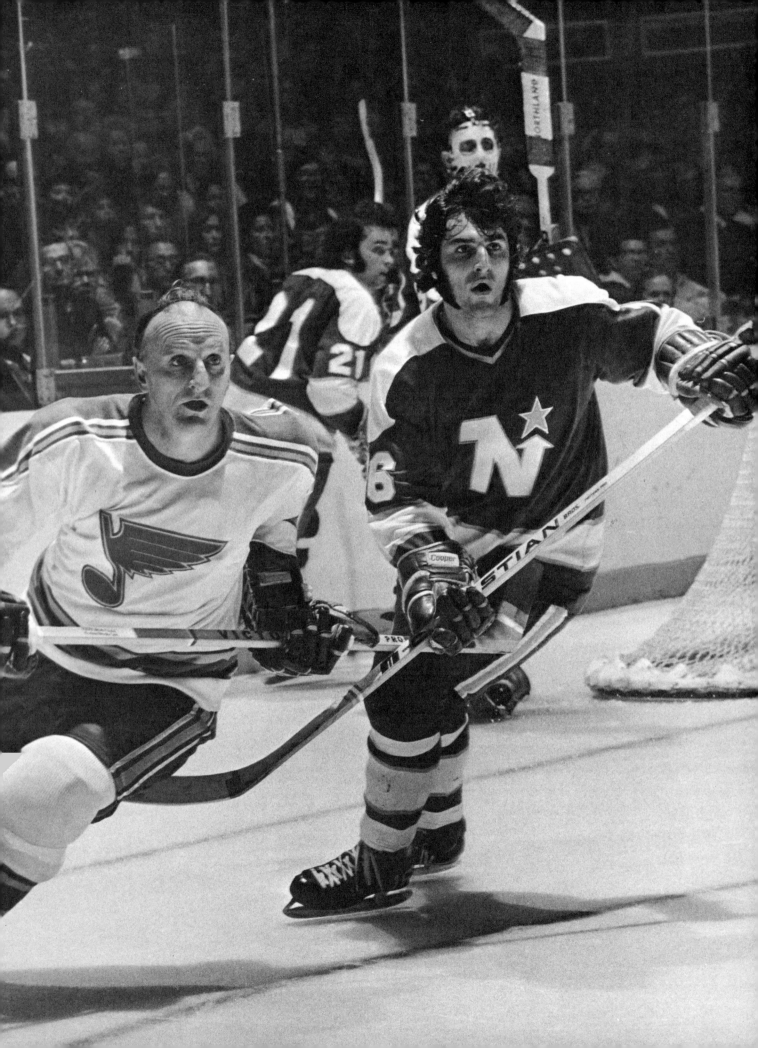

Jack Egers scans the horizon as the counterattack begins.

Emory Jones, a leading investment banker turned hockey operator, recalls the early days, when sellout crowds at the Arena were something hockey promoters only dreamed about.

"In the early days," Jones said, "when we didn't own the club, I still had to take charge of the receipts to make sure the players were paid. We had one fellow with a contract for $75 a week, and he told me he'd never got more than $30 cash before we came in."

The St. Louis operation was firmly handled by Jones, but the same couldn't be said for other clubs, such as Wichita.

"Wichita was supposed to open the season" said Jones, "and it didn't have any players. So the league president, William Grant, called me up and asked us [The Flyers] to go up and play in Wichita uniforms. A week later he asked us again, and we did. By the third week Wichita still didn't have a team and he called us once again. This time we couldn't go. I had to tell him *we* were playing *Wichita* that week!"

In the opening years of the 1940s there was no end in sight to the Flyers' superiority in the AHA. They finished first in 1940–41 and defeated St. Paul and then Kansas City in the playoffs. Although St. Louis finished atop the Northern Division of the AHA (in 1941–42 the league was split into two four-team divisions), that next season Omaha eliminated the Flyers in three consecutive games of the first playoff round.

By this time the United States as well as Canada was involved in World War II. Players from both countries had enlisted in their respective armed forces. The AHA was compelled to suspend operations. However, in 1944–45 the Flyers returned to the ice, although not too successfully. This time they were members of the powerful American Hockey League, and Emory Jones headed the club. The Flyers opened the season on October 27, 1944, at the Arena against the Cleveland Barons and set an attendance record as 13,384 fans poured through the turnstiles. They finished the season with a record of fourteen wins, eight ties, and thirty-eight losses, placing last in the AHL's Western Division.

Four years passed before the Flyers reached the top again; they made it in the 1948–49 season, leading the Western Division with an impressive record of forty-one victories, nine ties, and eighteen losses. It was the Flyers misfortune to meet powerful Providence, leaders of the Eastern Division, in the first round of the playoffs. The Rhode Island sextet finally eliminated St. Louis in the seventh and last game of the series by a score of 3–2.

A Popular Sport

More than 300,000 fans watched the Flyers that season, including 15,300 for a playoff game. Hockey was so popular in St. Louis that the AHL club actually outdrew the major league Browns of the American Baseball League. But the Flyers could never win the AHL playoffs.

Jones remembered how Providence always seemed to confound his team. One time St. Louis, facing the Rhode Islanders, needed only one victory to reach the postseason competition. "We were leading by one goal in the final seconds and had possession of the puck," said Jones. "A young fellow named Steve Black had the puck for us and was going down the ice. We could see he was going to try and score, and we knew we needed another goal like we needed a hole in the head.

"His teammate, Bill McComb, was racing along trying to catch him so he could freeze the puck. But Black shot the puck, which bounced off the Providence goalie's stick all the way back to the blue line. Providence scored and won the game in overtime!"

The Flyers lasted nine years in the AHL and then retired because of travel problems. Travel by train in those days was tedious and expensive. Cincinnati and Indianapolis already had dropped out, and the closest team city to St. Louis was Cleveland, 600 miles away.

In the intervening years, until the establishment of the Blues, fans in the Mound City would get a taste of big-league hockey every so often. It had become customary practice in hockey circles for teams to play "home" games in other cities. This would occur when the home rink was unavailable because of other commitments, or

The triumphant Kid line (l to r) Phil Roberto, Garry Unger and Mike Murphy.

The Gallery Gods speak out.

19

Chicago defenseman Keith Magnuson applies the stick to Frank St. Marseille.

when the novelty of the game in a hockeyless town would draw larger crowds than the home territory. Chicago's Black Hawks were having attendance problems between 1954 and 1956 and played several "home" games in St. Louis. In 1960 the Toledo-sextet of the International League finished its season at the Arena when the American Bowling Congress tournament took over its home arena.

In 1962 the Syracuse franchise of the Eastern Hockey League finished its campaign in St. Louis, where it switched to the Central Professional Hockey League. A Chicago Black Hawks farm team, they were renamed the St. Louis Braves. The Braves developed future NHL stars, such as Phil Esposito and Doug Jarrett, who learned their trade there under the coaching of former big-league defenseman Gus Kyle.

The Braves were an attractive addition to the Mound City's sport scene, but hardly befitted a major league metropolis. However, their activities set the stage for the eventual decision to once again place major league hockey in St. Louis on a permanent basis.

The Bruins have been repulsed. Now for the counterattack

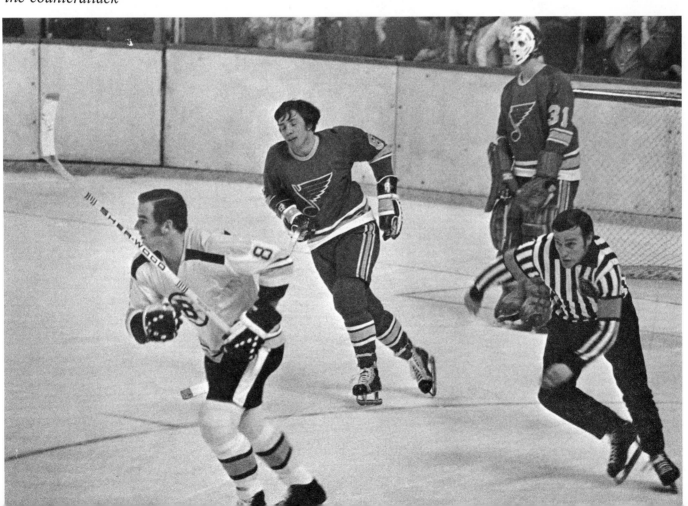

The builder of the Blues—Sid Salomon III.

the salomon's magic touch

Even with such a rich hockey heritage, St. Louis was not considered a favorite to gain entry to the National Hockey League when, in 1965, the league finally voted to expand from six to twelve teams. The franchise price was $2,000,000, and twenty-four groups representing twelve cities bid for the honor of having a major league hockey team.

Within a year, five cities were admitted—Los Angeles, Minneapolis-St. Paul, Pittsburgh, Philadelphia, and Oakland. Still out in the cold, St. Louis, if it hoped to gain entry, would have to outbid Vancouver, Buffalo, and Baltimore, among others.

*Stanley Cup action. Gary Sabourin's shot
rolls past Boston goalie Gerry Cheevers.*

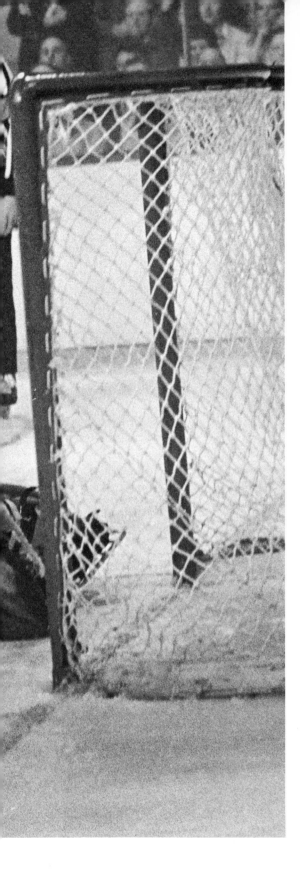

When the final decision had to be made, St. Louis was able to present some overwhelming assets. It had a completed arena that fulfilled the NHL's requirement that there be at least 12,500 seats; it had the support of the Chicago Black Hawks, which owned the St. Louis Arena; and it had a purchasing group with the highest credentials, which was headed by Sidney Salomon, Jr. and his son, Sidney Salomon III.

Sidney, Jr. knew sports from every angle. He was a $125-a-month sportswriter for the old *St. Louis Times* in 1929 at the age of 19. He later entered the insurance business, and the firm flourished under his aegis. He also became intensely interested in politics.

In time he became treasurer of the Democratic National Committee, but not before being involved in one of the turning points in modern American history.

"Salomon," said NHL president Clarence Campbell, "swung the 1944 Democratic convention to putting Harry Truman on the ballot as vice-president instead of Henry Wallace. In Salomon, we've got a genuine king-maker."

Truman, of course, became vice-president and then president following the death of Franklin Delano Roosevelt in 1945. Salomon's interest in politics didn't wane, and in 1960 he became chairman of fund-raising for the successful John F. Kennedy-Lyndon B. Johnson Democratic campaign.

Meanwhile the Salomon family also maintained an avid interest in sports. Sidney, Jr., who excelled at golf, won an amateur championship. He served on the board of directors of the old St. Louis Browns as well as on the board of the Cardinals. He bought the Syracuse team of the International League and moved it to Miami in 1955, thereby giving the family sufficient sports-operational experience to help in making the new team a success.

"The Birth of the Blues"

On April 6, 1966, the NHL Board of Governors granted St. Louis the franchise. In no time at all the team was nicknamed "The Blues." Then the Arena was purchased from Arthur Wirtz, owner of the Chicago Black Hawks, for $4,000,000.

The Salomons were responsible for several monumental improvements in the St. Louis sports scene, but none compare with the multi-million dollar renaissance of the Arena. In a matter of months the classic building received a complete face-lifting, inside and out. By opening night it was superior in both design and construction to the other ultra-modern structures which house the NHL teams.

Replacing the old façade was a gleaming entrance of white trimmed in gold and old brick, capped by a unique and colorful sign hailing the "Home of the BLUES." The ticket windows were moved from their former outdoor location to new positions inside the widened lobby. Press facilities were updated, and a private Arena club and a dazzling Walnut Room gave a new tone of dignity to the sports facilities. Other improvements included theater-type seats, a modern score clock, an improved lighting system, and better parking facilities, all adding to increased enjoyment of the game.

The First Season

Seating 14,500, the "new" Arena opened for the regular 1967–68 season on October 11, 1967, when 11,339 fans came out to watch big league hockey once again. Celebrities such as Arthur Godfrey, Anna Marie Alberghetti, and Guy Lombardo were on hand when the Blues tied the Minnesota North Stars 2–2. The honor of scoring the first St. Louis goal went to forward Larry Keenan.

Meanwhile the Salomons continued to explore every possible method to make hockey a success in St. Louis. "Treat your employes with respect," was their motto, "keep them happy, and give the public full value for its money."

Producing a winner was one of the top priorities. To do so, the Salomons hired Lynn Patrick, with long experience as an NHL player, coach and manager. He was appointed manager-coach, and Scotty Bowman became assistant manager and coach. Thanks to the league draft,

Witness for the defense. Minnesota defenseman Barry Gibbs guards Garry Unger during the 1972 playoffs.

Organist extraordinaire—Norm Kramer.

they obtained Glenn Hall from Chicago—otherwise known as "Mister Goalie"—first and built a team around him. Veterans such as Ron Stewart, Jim Roberts, Don McKenney, and Al Arbour were signed, as well as a large sprinkling of youngsters such as Terry Crisp, Gary Sabourin, Tim Ecclestone, and Frank St. Marseille.

Organist Norm Kramer

A seemingly inconspicuous addition to the Blues family was organist Norm Kramer, who eventually became a catalyst for St. Louis hockey victories. One NHL coach claimed that Kramer automatically added a goal to the Blues side just by being there.

Kramer had been a hockey buff, confining himself to seats far from the rink in the old Arena hockey days. One day while entertaining in an Italian restaurant, Emory Jones discovered him. When the Blues were looking for someone to play the organ for the first season, they auditioned Kramer who played "The St. Louis Blues" so enthusiastically that Sid Salomon Jr. signed him to a contract.

Kramer's wit and enthusiasm were soon transferred to the keys and on to the crowd.

"It was like a chain reaction," says Lynn Patrick. "Norm would play, the crowd would react by picking up the chant, and the team would catch fire."

Kramer's repertoire for fight chants built up week by week. One night St. Louis trailed Minnesota 3–0 and appeared hopelessly out of the game when Patrick dispatched a note to Kramer.

"Lynn asked me to play 'When The Saints Go Marching In.' He said the team seems to rise up when they hear it," Norm relates.

The final score was Blues 5, North Stars 3.

Pain and Progress

As an ancient philosopher once said, pain and progress are inseparable; and the Blues experienced their share of pain in that rookie year.

Collision of the superstars—Brad Park
(l) and Garry Unger.

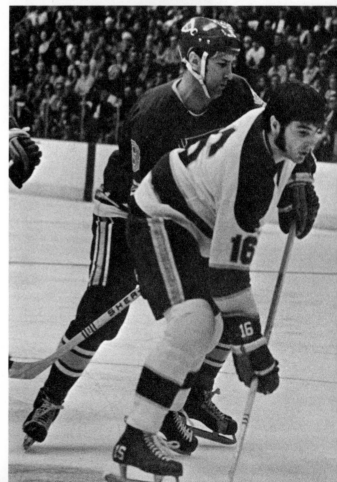

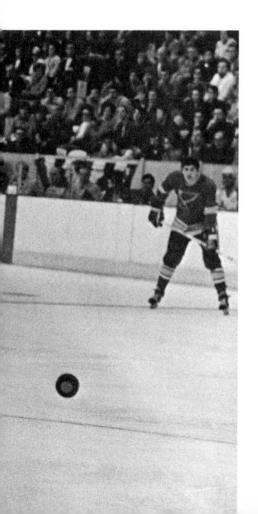

"We worked and planned and sweated all that first summer of 1967," says Sid Salomon, Jr. "We kept telling ourselves that everything would be fine, but maybe we were whistling to keep up our courage."

Certainly the Salomons required all the courage they could muster in the first half of the 1967–68 campaign. Crowds thinned out after the opening game, and although Glenn Hall performed weekly miracles in goal—St. Louis defeated Boston 5–1 on November 1, 1967, at the Arena—by November 22 the Blues were in the West Division cellar, and Patrick turned the coaches reins over to Bowman. On November 26, St. Louis lost its seventh straight game, and concern was rampant throughout the front office.

The Blues visited Madison Square Garden on November 26 and were beaten 1–0 by the Rangers. More important than that, however, was a meeting between New York manager-coach Emile Francis and the Blues high command. Francis had been unhappy with the performance of center Gordon "Red" Berenson, a University of Michigan graduate with esoteric interests. Francis, who had never completed high school, lost touch with Berenson and frowned upon Red's intellectual approach to life.

"If I ever see Berenson read a book on the bus again," Francis once confided to a reporter, "I'm going to throw him off!"

Francis apparently felt that Red should be spending more time communing with his teammates to the betterment of his game.

Francis finally threw Berenson off the Rangers, dispatching him to St. Louis on November 27 along with Barclay Plager, brother of Bob Plager, in return for Ron Stewart who had been the Blues' leading scorer, and Ron Attwell. It turned out to be one of the most one-sided trades in hockey history. With the Blues, Berenson scored 22 goals, read all the books on the team buses that he pleased, and was voted West Division "Player of the Year" by the *Sporting News*.

Larry Ziegler behind the bench.

The Magic Touch

Suddenly every move made by the Salomons and their staff seemed to have the magic touch. On December 3 they persuaded former Montreal Canadiens ace Dickie Moore to come out of retirement, and a week later Moore scored the winning goal in a 2–1 upset victory over the Toronto Maple Leafs.

"By now," says Patrick, "I thought we had a good club. The veterans held up well, and the rookies came along fast."

So did the fans. An appreciative audience of 13,873 turned out on January 27, 1968 to watch the Blues overcome a 3–0 deficit and defeat the Rangers 4–3 on Bill McCreary's goal with 11:56 remaining in the game. A month later St. Louis rallied from a 3–0 score against Montreal and tied the vaunted Canadiens 3–3. This time Frank St. Marseille was the hero, scoring the tying goal.

If Berenson was a surprise asset so was Barclay Plager, who came west with the redhead from New York. Along with brother Bob, big Noel Picard, and Al Arbour, they gave St. Louis one of the most dreaded blue line corps in the NHL.

The bespectacled Arbour, who eventually became coach and then assistant general manager of the Blues, emerged as the league's unsung hero defenseman.

"I don't think there's anyone I'd rather have playing in front of me than Arbour," said Glenn Hall. "He's the most underrated defenseman in the league. No one is better at blocking shots, and he's got perfect timing."

Aiming High

Having vacated the West Division cellar, the Blues now aimed high, and the Arena crowds climbed along with them. On March 2, 1968, the regular season's largest turnout, 15,351, saw the Blues take on Chicago's Black Hawks. Although the visitors jumped ahead by two goals, St. Louis rallied and thoroughly exhilirated the home crowd by tying Chicago 3–3.

In the homestretch, the Blues sprinted past Minnesota with back-to-back victories over the North Stars and captured third place. Typically, St. Louis rallied in each case. On Saturday night, at the Arena, a pair of goals by Larry Keenan in the last two-and-a-half minutes earned the victory. The next night the Blues scored three last period goals at Metropolitan Sports Center for a 5–3 win.

To the Playoffs

For the first time in St. Louis hockey history, the team was to participate in the Stanley Cup playoffs. First-place Philadelphia would be the opening round foe and, naturally, the favorite. A pulsating, often brutal series, the playoff with the Flyers established a rivalry between Philadelphia and St. Louis that remains one of the most bitter in all sports.

It began on April 4, 1968, when the Blues defeated Philadelphia 1–0 at the Spectrum on Jimmy Roberts' goal. The Flyers tied the series, but St. Louis went ahead once more when Keenan scored in the second sudden-death overtime for a 3–2 triumph on April 10. Scotty Bowman's skaters followed up with a 5–2 rout on April 11 and had the series in their grasp when Philadelphia rallied to win the next two matches and force a seventh and final game on April 18 at the hostile Spectrum. Reeling from loss of momentum, the Blues needed something, or someone, to straighten them out. That turned out to be Doug Harvey, the former Canadiens defenseman who had been player-coach for the Blues' Kansas City farm team during the regular season. He had been sprung loose when Kansas City was eliminated from the Central League playoffs.

Harvey was pressed into service for the seventh game and played like the ten-time First All-Star that he had been in earlier years. With the score tied 1–1 in the second period, Harvey skimmed a perfect pass to Keenan who went in and scored the winning goal. Berenson shot the insurance point into the open net in the final minute of play. Now the cry in the Blues' dressing room was "Bring on the North Stars!"

Face-off! Garry Unger vs. Red Berenson, central figures in the big deal of 1971.

32

Now the North Stars

It seemed impossible for the effervescent Blues to top the Philadelphia series for sheer metabolic turmoil, but the Minnesota-St. Louis confrontation had all the exciting elements of the Philadelphia series, and then some. Once again the teams seemed to be on a roller coaster; up one game and down the next. With the teams tied at three games each, the seventh game of the series would determine the final outcome. This time the seventh game extended into an excruciatingly thrilling sudden-death overtime.

The teams battled back and forth through the first 20-minute extra period without result. A record Arena crowd of 15,566 was contracting a massive case of laryngitis as the second overtime period opened. Then, as so frequently happens in a sport as unpredictable as hockey, a virtual unknown emerged as the hero of heroes.

The man of the hour was big, blond, 23-year-old Ron Schock, who had scored a paltry 9 goals in 55 regular season games, and who had been regarded as one of the more disappointing skaters on the Blues. What's more, Schock had done absolutely nothing in the playoffs. Nothing, that is, until the two-and-a-half-minute mark of the second sudden death. Accepting passes from Bill McCreary and Gerry Melnyk, Shock flashed past the North Stars' bewildered defense and skated on a head-on course towards North Star goalie Cesare Maniago. Schock shot and Maniago lunged, but he was too late. The Blues were the winners, 2–1, and had qualified for the Stanley Cup finals against the mighty Montreal Canadiens.

The Flying Frenchmen and the Finals

Based on the relatives merits of both teams, the Flying Frenchmen could be expected not only to sweep St. Louis in four straight games but were considered strong enough to win every match by about five goals. This was not to be quite the case. While they did win the series in four games, the doughty Blues twice took them into overtime before losing. More to St. Louis' credit, the

Boston goalie Gerry Cheevers blunts an attack.

It takes courage to be a hockey player, but a special brand of guts is necessary to play the game while wearing glasses. Al Arbour had just that kind of intestinal fortitude. He earned the rich accolade, "The Defenseman's Defenseman!" And he is earning new accolades as team coach.

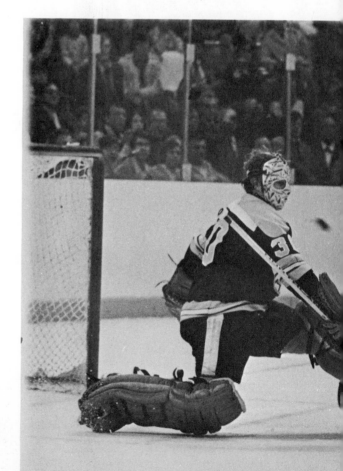

Blues were outscored only eleven to seven. They had also received such superior goaltending from Glenn Hall that "Mister Goalie" was voted the Conn Smythe Trophy as the most valuable player in the Cup round.

The Salomon success story registered at the gate as well as on the ice. Including the playoffs, the Blues attracted 455,000 fans, a remarkable figure considering that the St. Louis Cardinals didn't pass that mark until their first pennant-winning season of 1926.

It soon became evident that the Blues' extraordinary effort was traceable not only to the players' outstanding abilities but also to some special motivating forces that the Salomons were able to produce. One strong motivating factor was the fact that they paid their players higher salaries and bonuses than most of the other teams. For this Sid, Jr. was criticized by such conservative hockey mogul types as the then Toronto Maple Leafs general manager-coach Punch Imlach. Salomon had the perfect squelch for this kind of criticism.

"I think it's my business," he replied. "I am simply showing my appreciation for the thrills and satisfaction the Blues give me. Bringing big-league hockey back to St. Louis has been a great reward for me."

St. Louis sports fans responded during the off-season with a welling demand for season tickets; one that surprised young Sid Salomon III, who had watched the subscription requests reach 9,000 long before the 1968–69 season was to start.

A Generous Management

Such overwhelming popularity presented a peculiar problem prior to the opening game against the Los Angeles Kings. Only 1,000 tickets remained for the premiere when the box office manager informed young Salomon that he had 1,000 orders for the three-dollar seats, which had already been sold out. Salomon's solution was to give 800 of the four-dollar seats to the first customers who had requested the threes.

"We told them," said Sid III, "that we were making the extra dollar an opening night present."

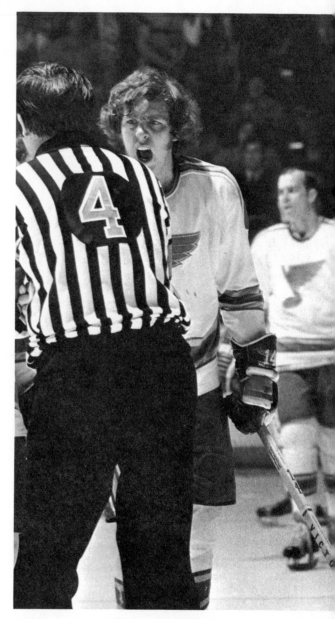

"You need a pair of glasses!"

Textbook stickhandling; the puck is manipulated with the right hand while the left hand fends off the enemy.

The essence of hockey action—lyrical speed.

Former captain Red Berenson.

Not unusual was the gift from the Salomons of an inscribed gold watch worth $750 to tiny Camille Henry in appreciation of his scoring the first three-goal hat trick ever netted by a Blues player.

"This," says Henry, "is something I'll always treasure, because it's one of the few things I've ever received from hockey."

Henry's reward was small potatoes compared with the cornucopia of gifts the Salomon's bestowed upon Red Berenson during the 1968–69 season for his unique scoring spree. The man they had come to call "The Red Baron" was not only given a watch similar to Henry's but a shotgun and a station wagon with a canoe sitting on the roof.

In earning these prizes, Berenson did something no other NHL player has done to date in modern big-league hockey history. He scored six goals in one game. These were netted on the night of November 7, 1968, against the Philadelphia Flyers at the Spectrum, as the Blues won 8–0. Four of Red's goals were scored in one period, tying another league record. Even so Berenson, along with the rest of the hockey world, was astonished by the Salomon's generosity.

"It could only happen here in St. Louis," he said after a special "night" was held in his honor. "Not that I was looking for anything like this, but in Montreal or New York, where I had played earlier in my career, all you could expect for six goals was a pat on the back!"

In return for their generosity, the Salomons received the brand of hockey normally expected of high-class established clubs. Soon after "l'affaire Berenson," the Blues played the Bruins to a 1–1 tie at Boston Garden, whipped the Rangers 3–1 at Madison Square Garden, and tied Detroit 1–1 in St. Louis with the Red Wings just barely obtaining the draw with a goal in the final minute of play.

Atop the Division

Only a year earlier St. Louis had been mired in last place; now they were most emphatically atop the West

Red Berenson in many kinds of action.

Division. Only a year before empty seats had been visible at all home games; now it was impossible to find an empty seat in the Arena. When the Blues returned from a six-game road trip late in November, 1968, a standing-room-only crowd of 15,117 jammed the Arena, raising the attendance average to 13,500 for the first seven home games, only two of which were against established teams.

The Blues were winning friends and luring crowds because they had achieved that all-important show business mystique—star-quality. Red Berenson became the first expansion skater to grace the cover of America's leading sports magazine. He had become the West Division's first authentic superstar. But Berenson alone couldn't make a winning team. The Salomons, Lynn Patrick, and Scotty Bowman had realized that good goaltending spells the difference between winning and losing. So putting together an effective one-two goaltending combination had been a top priority before the opening of the 1968–69 season.

Getting the Goalies

Getting goalies was not easy, especially since the 37-year-old Glenn Hall had toyed with retirement, and 39-year-old Jacques Plante, the other object of the Blues' goaltending affections, had "retired" from the NHL in 1965. To persuade Hall to return, Bowman employed an interesting stratagem. He phoned the goaltender at his 80-acre farm in Stony Plain, Alberta, but spoke first with Hall's son Pat. Scotty learned that Hall had been in splendid health and spirits and then asked that Pat put his father on the phone.

The moment Glenn picked up the receiver, Bowman declared, "So you're returning, eh?"

Taken aback, Hall replied, "Who says?"

"Your son," snapped Bowman.

The best Hall could answer then was, "Oh!" Naturally, he was back with the Blues for 1968–69 but with one significant change; for the first time in his career Hall wore a face mask.

"I want to be sure I can collect my paycheck personally from now on," he explained. "I don't want it mailed to the Good Samaritan Hospital . . . or to the cemetery."

The Salomons didn't have to lure Plante out of retirement; he really *wanted* to play. And when he learned about the generosity of the Blues' front office, he was appropriately amazed.

Plante said, "I never dreamed of getting a salary like this [approximately $35,000]."

In like fashion, the Blues hadn't dreamed of getting the eminently superior goaltending that they were to receive from the old master—although Bowman had never doubted that Plante, despite his absence from the NHL, could handle the job. Bowman knew that Plante had quit because his wife had been ill, not because he couldn't perform. He told Plante that they would play him in no less than 30 games, nor in more than 40. Plante was impressed with Bowman's straightforwardness.

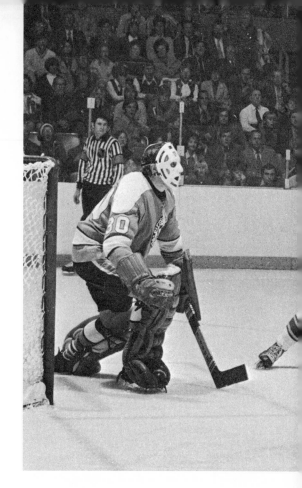

Outstanding Goalkeeping

Bowman made good on his promise and used Plante in 37 games. In turn, Plante allowed a miserly 70 goals for a 1.96 goals against average; the kind most NHL goaltenders spend their lives dreaming about. As an added fillip, Plante recorded five shutouts and collaborated perfectly with Hall. "Mister Goalie" was also at the top of his game, scoring a league-leading eight shutouts and a neat 2.17 goals against average.

Hall and Plante captured the Vezina Trophy for the Blues and were the principal reason St. Louis ran away with the West Division race. On March 8, 1969, the Blues defeated the Seals 5–2 at the Arena to clinch first place, which entitled them to the Clarence Campbell Bowl. The season officially ended on March 29, at which time the St. Louis Blues led the West Division with a healthy 19 points between them and the second place California Seals.

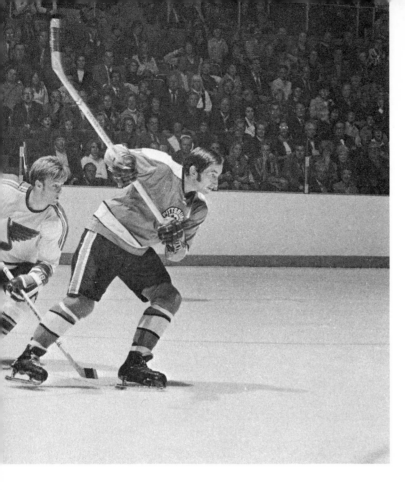

Floyd Thomson cuts between Pittsburgh goalie Les Binkley and defenseman Bob Woytowich.

Frank St. Marseille (l) and Gary Sabourin stare the puck into the Vancouver net.

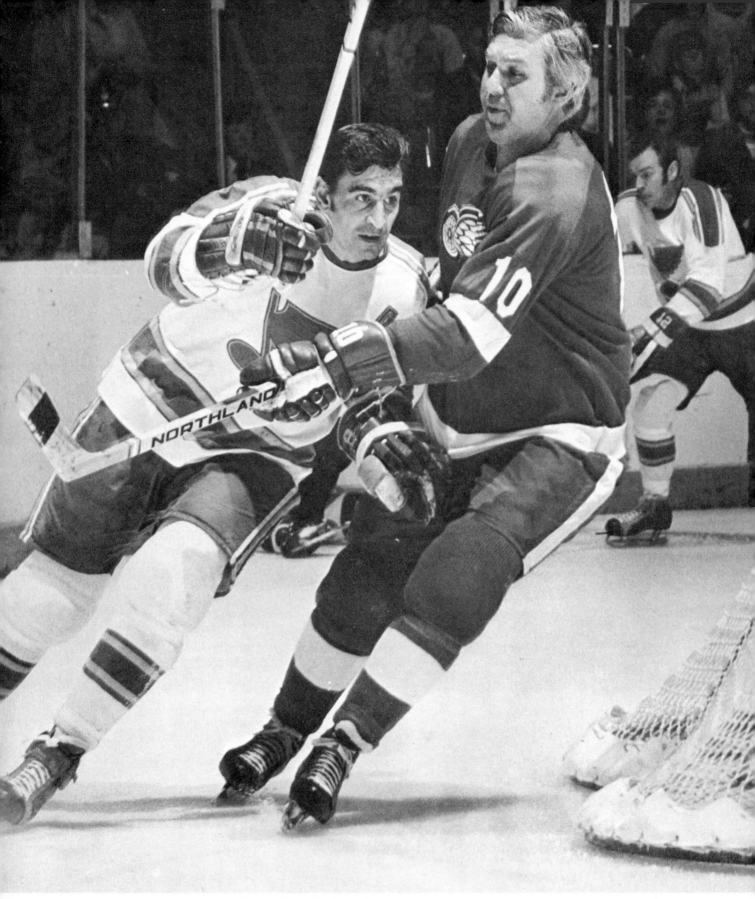

Red Wings captain Alex Delvecchio guards the irrepressible Barclay Plager.

The Secret of Success

"The secret," said coach Bowman, "is to put together the best of the old coaching techniques, because there aren't too many new coaching methods. Lynn Patrick has taught me a lot in the years we've been together. In fact, some of the techniques we use were first introduced by his father, Lester, when he coached the old New York Rangers."

A sprinkling of veterans such as Doug Harvey, Hall, and Plante, gave St. Louis maturity, but the Blues also had plenty of youngsters. Among them were players such as Gary Sabourin, the Plager Brothers, Ron Schock, Craig Cameron, and Tim Ecclestone.

Even though Hall was injured at playoff time the Blues combination was a winner. They humbled the Philadelphia Flyers in four straight games of the opening Stanley Cup round and then went up against the Los Angeles Kings.

At first it appeared that the California sextet would be a bother. Although the Blues took the first game 4–0, and Berenson tied the NHL playoff record with three goals in one period, the Kings battled fiercely in the second match. They held the Blues to a 2–2 tie until Sabourin scored a third and winning goal. That finished Los Angeles. The Blues jetted to the West Coast and swept the next two games at the Forum at Inglewood, California. Once again the St. Louis Blues faced the Montreal Canadiens in the Stanley Cup finals.

"I know it's going to be tough in the finals," said Bowman, "but we're proud of ourselves. You've really got to have something to win eight straight games."

No matter what the Blues did against Montreal, their performance against Philadelphia and Los Angeles was the talk of the West Division.

"Checking and defense was the difference," said Red Kelly, then coach of the Kings. "The St. Louis defense was smarter and sharper than ours, and they gave the puck away a lot less."

The Canadiens Again

Although they made a fight of it, handling the star-studded Canadiens was a bit too much for the Blues. Montreal captured the first two games at the Forum by identical 3–1 scores. The third game was a real disappointment, as a record standing-room-only St. Louis crowd saw the Blues shut out by Rogatien Vachon 4–0. Terry Gray scored the game's first goal on May 4 in the finale, but the indomitable Canadiens eventually tied the game and won it 2–1 to annex the Stanley Cup.

Nevertheless, by now St. Louis sports fans had taken the Blues to their collective hearts, and the Salomons now took the fans to *their* hearts. During the off-season more than 12,000 new, comfortable plastic contoured seats replaced older chairs in the Arena, and seating capacity for hockey was increased to 15,500.

"I want to give the fans a building they could be proud of," said Sid Salomon, Jr. "We might as well do it right and let the fans know we aren't out to make a fast buck."

Other improvements included a pair of 40-foot-long moving message panels which flashed simultaneous information in three-foot-high illuminated letters on either side of the Arena. The message boards were attached to newly built sky boxes adorning the Arena's interior. Heating and ventilating systems were improved, rest rooms were added, and new furnishings decorated the lobby. New names began to appear on the Blues roster. Within three weeks of June, 1969, the wheeling and dealing of Patrick and Bowman added forwards André Boudrias, Wayne Maki, Ron Anderson, and Bob Schmautz to the lineup, along with goalie Ernie Wakely, among others.

Smooth As Silk Goyette

One of the most surprising and beneficial additions was 35-year-old chain-smoking center Phil Goyette, whom the Blues obtained from the New York Rangers. Despite his age and the fact that the Rangers had deemed him expendable, Goyette, who is now coach of

The classic kick save, a la Jacques Caron.

the New York Islanders, had plenty of good hockey left in him, and all of that was extracted by the St. Louis scene.

"If the Rangers had traded me to any other team," said Goyette, "I might have retired. But, like everyone in the league, I'd heard that the St. Louis owners were good to their players and the working conditions were above average. Actually, it's kind of hard to believe."

The same could be said of Goyette's performance, which amazed fans and players alike.

"I can't say that I've ever seen a better playmaker," said experienced forward Ab McDonald. "Goyette is as smooth as silk."

McDonald spoke first-hand. He and winger Ron Anderson teamed up with Goyette to give the Blues a potent scoring line that once again lifted St. Louis to the top of the West Division.

"I'm not a goal-scorer," said the modest Goyette, "I'm a playmaker. If my wingers score, I look good. If they don't . . ."

Despite his protestations Goyette scored 29 goals—second highest on the Blues—and 49 assists for a team-leading 78 points in seventy-two games. The Blues finished first in the West Division by a commanding 22 points over second-place Pittsburgh and then defeated both the Minnesota North Stars and Pittsburgh Penguins in six games each in the Stanley Cup first and second round respectively.

The Finals Once More

This time, instead of facing the Montreal Canadiens the Blues went up against a new opponent in the finals, the Boston Bruins. But if the foe was different, the result was the same. St. Louis dropped the first three games by decisive margins—6–1, 6–2, 4–1—but gave the big, bad Bruins a run for their money in the fourth and telling game on May 10, 1970. At the end of regulation time the teams were tied 3–3, and the Blues appeared close to ending their non-winning Cup final jinx. Unfortunately, superstar Bobby Orr had other ideas and lifted a sudden-death goal over Glenn Hall, giving Boston the Stanley Cup.

The "alternate" goaltenders—Garry Unger (l) and Bob Plager.

However, even in defeat the Blues could hold their heads high. They had won the Clarence S. Campbell Bowl for two consecutive years and were clearly the class team of the West Division. Moreover, the Salomons had created a positive attitude about the Blues that excited the hockey world.

"There's a different atmosphere in St. Louis," said Goyette. "You want to work harder. Naturally, the ownership has something to do with it. The Salomons mix with the players more than most owners. They give you the impression that you're part of the organization. There's something special about playing for the Blues.

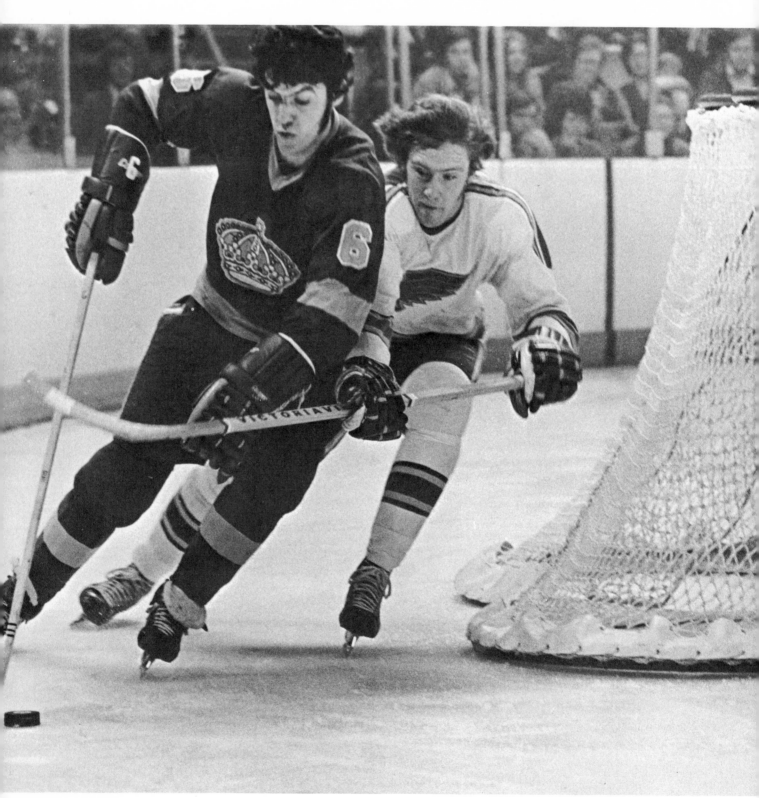

The art of forechecking.

the old order changeth

Stung by the Blues' failure to win a playoff game against an established team, the St. Louis high command understood that changes would have to be made if the Blues were to remain competitive in the West Division now that the Chicago Black Hawks had been switched from East to West for the 1970–71 season.

"We've got the best fans in the league," said Scotty Bowman, "the best owners in the league, and the best franchise in the league. Unfortunately, we don't have the best team in the league. To get that, we've got to get more players like Red Berenson and Bobby Orr. We have to draft the top young players coming out of Canada each year. But the higher you finish the lower you draft, and that makes it tough to improve yourself.

But if there's a way to improve the Blues, we'll find it. Just you wait and see.''

As the 1970–71 season unfolded, it became apparent that the Blues still were the finest of the expansion teams. But with Chicago in the West Division, St. Louis had to be content with second place, and weaknesses soon betrayed themselves in the lineup. By far the most glaring was Berenson's inability to maintain his point-a-game average of previous years. Even worse, the Red Baron was not scoring goals. After 45 games, Berenson had only 16 goals. The time had come to improve the club.

Exit Berenson—Enter Unger

As luck would have it, the Detroit Red Wings were as disenchanted with their promising center, Garry Unger, as the Blues were with Berenson. Negotiations between the Red Wings and Blues were opened, and on February 6, 1971, Berenson and forward Tim Ecclestone were traded to Detroit for Unger and forward Wayne Connolly.

Reaction was divided as to which team benefitted most by the trade. Some Detroiters seemed to feel the Blues had received the best of the bargain.

News of the deal resounded through St. Louis with the impact of a thunderclap. Blues fans were openly dismayed about the departure of The Red Baron and hardly enthused about the blond, long-haired Unger.

"I don't blame the fans," said Sid Salomon III. "If I were on their side of the fence, I'd probably be writing or phoning my criticism. But we weren't trading for today, tomorrow, or the next NHL season. We were dealing for the next ten years. We believe Unger is the kind of man we need to build a Stanley Cup-winner."

"We got a hockey player with a great future in Unger," said Scotty Bowman in agreement.

Impartial observers said that Unger's problem in Detroit was that Garry was too hip for conservative manager Ned Harkness. When Unger checked into the Red Wings' training camp that autumn, Harkness had

Poetry in motion—Jack Egers.

Phil Roberto pursues Minnesota defense-
man Barry Gibbs while North Stars goalie
Gump Worsley blocks the cage.

blanched at the sight of his abundant blond hair and ordered Garry to trim his lengthy locks. Unger complied, but not enough to suit Harkness. Three more visits to the barber shop were ordered by the manager.

"In my opinion," said Unger, "the length of my hair was irrelevant to hockey."

The Blues' management shared that philosophy. Garry finished the 1970-71 season with the most beautiful coiffed head in the NHL and 15 goals, 14 assists, for 29 points in twenty-eight games, just the point-a-game average the Blues had not received from Berenson. Also gratifying to management was the corroboration of the correctness of their decision, since Berenson had managed 17 points in twenty-four games with Detroit.

Better still, the St. Louis fans developed a growing appreciation of Unger with each passing game. His long, flowing hair contrasted with the helmeted Berenson and suggested a certain joie de vivre about Garry that enthralled the fans. And besides, he could score. Garry led the Blues in scoring during the first round playoff against Minnesota for the 1971 Stanley Cup, but the Blues could not cope with an aroused North Stars team which knocked them out of the series in six games.

More Changes

This sudden exit suggested that more changes would have to be made. They were. Scotty Bowman departed to become coach of the Montreal Canadiens, and he was replaced by Sid Abel, the 53-year-old former coach and manager of the Red Wings.

It didn't take Abel very long to realize that he faced an awesome task. The retirement of Glenn Hall left the Blues without a superior veteran goaltender for the first time since the club was organized.

"We have," said Abel, "a definite problem in the nets."

Defense was less of a problem. The Plager Brothers and Noel Picard had returned, and Carl Brewer was obtained from Detroit.

"Knowing how well Carl can move the puck out of our zone," said Abel, "is a comfort."

The manager, Sid Abel.

Up front the Blues had a surplus of centers, including speedy young Gene Carr, who had been obtained via the amateur draft. But Abel wondered just who would become the new leader now that Berenson was gone. He felt that it might be Unger, who was well thought of by the fans and could do all the things a hockey player is supposed to do.

Not much went well for St. Louis in the first month of the 1971–72 campaign. The Blues just barely escaped the West Division cellar. A coaching change seemed to be in order. Abel, who hadn't found the winning combination, was promoted to general manager. General manager Lynn Patrick was named vice-president, and former defensive ace Bill McCreary was imported from Denver of the Western League to coach the Blues. Meanwhile, troubles continued to pile up, one of the worst of which was a horseback-riding accident to veteran defenseman Noel Picard, who came out of it with a mangled foot.

In his new position as manager, Abel began making a series of deals that would drastically change the shape of the Blues. His first major move was to send Gene Carr, Jim Lorentz, and Wayne Connelly to the Rangers in exchange for wingers Jack "Smoky" Egers and Mike Murphy and husky, tough defenseman André "Moose" Dupont.

"We now have passed the time when it will be good enough to be the best of the expansionists," said Abel. "We have to look to the time when we can compete with the Establishment equally. Everyone seems sympathetic to our problems and we are enjoying marvelous support. Hockey interest in St. Louis seems as keen as ever."

Turning It Around

Abel was right. Attendance at the Arena was greater than ever, which caused the fan-oriented Salomons distress over the Blues' inability to climb under the leadership of McCreary. After 24 games with the new coach, St. Louis recorded six wins, four ties and fourteen

Goalie Jacques Plante, now a Maple Leaf, foils his former team.

Guarded by Boston defenseman Dallas Smith, Barclay Plager passes to a teammate.

defeats. On Christmas Day, 1971, McCreary was replaced by Al Arbour.

Almost obscured by that announcement was another significant exchange. The Blues had traded 31-year-old captain Jim Roberts to Montreal for 23-year-old forward Phil Roberto. These various changes would, in time, turn it all around for the Blues.

A New Confidence

As difficult as the trading, wheeling, and dealing may have been, they did alter the Blues outlook from defeatism to a new self-assurance that would take them to a playoff berth. The transformation took time but was speeded, ironically enough, by a bizarre incident at Philadelphia's Spectrum, when several Blues were attacked by Flyers fans. A brouhaha ensued which brought in the Philadelphia police force. The end result was the development of a new esprit de corps among the Blues that catapulted them right back into the West Division playoff race.

Perhaps most gratifying of all was the evolvement of a scoring line that was among the best in either division. The Whiz Kids—Garry Unger, Mike Murphy, and Jack Egers—developed into a goaltender's nightmare. Egers's shot had the velocity usually associated with Bobby Hull's bombs. The rookie Murphy looked right at home speeding up and down right wing, and Unger became the ideal playmaker at center.

"We'll get better," said Unger, "the longer we're together."

"We usually like to get two guys in on the goal," Murphy explained, "and one guy back. I like to go into those corners."

"All of the great lines in the NHL have been together for a long time," said Egers. "I hope that we can stay together."

They got better and they stayed together. As a result, the Blues lifted themselves into a third place finish, although they were 19 points behind second place Minnesota, the team they would face in the opening playoff round.

His stick at the charging position, Gary Sabourin heads back to his defensive goal.

the great playoff upset

Throughout the 1971–72 season, the Blues found themselves in the unaccustomed position of underdogs. In the middle of the campaign Philadelphia Flyers manager Keith Allen and Philly coach Fred Shero told the hockey world that there was no way the Blues could even make the playoffs.

"They said," coach Al Arbour recalled, "that no matter what changes we made, we still weren't good enough to beat them out because we just didn't have the personnel."

Yet it was the Flyers who finished in fifth place, out of the Stanley Cup round, and the Blues who skated against the heavily favored Minnesota North Stars.

Once again put-downs were hurled at the Mound City skaters. "The North Stars think we're afraid of them," said Garry Unger. "They think they're going to skate over a bunch of kids."

One reason for the Minnesota optimism was the North Stars' record of four wins out of six meetings with the Blues. Yet an overlooked set of statistics that eventually would prove significant was the respective records of both teams during the last half of the schedule. The younger Blues had an 18–15–4 record for 40 points. Minnesota, an older club, was 14–16–7 for 35 points.

Even though most Minnesota players expressed optimism, the oldest North Star, 42-year-old goalie Lorne "Gump" Worsley, spoke prudently and prophetically as the teams prepared for the series' first game on April 5, 1972, at Metropolitan Sports Center in Bloomington, Minnesota.

"I'm looking for a long, tough series. There's no such thing as a favorite or underdog in the playoffs. It's like starting a new season—everybody's equal."

If so, you couldn't tell it from the action in the opener. Playing before an overflowing and enthusiastic home crowd, the North Stars came out like Gang Busters and smote the Blues 3–0. Even when Minnesota was compelled to play two men short due to penalties early in the game, St. Louis' power play was impotent.

"If we could have scored then," said coach Arbour, "the outcome might have been different. We just couldn't capitalize. We were overanxious, trying to do too many things at the same time."

When the North Stars' defense weakened, Worsley was more than equal to the task. And when the Gumper wasn't good, he was lucky. Early in the third period Unger fired a bomb that was so hot the puck bounced out of Worsley's glove. But it hit the goal post and bounced out of danger.

Sudden Death

As a result, the Blues were delighted to see Cesare Maniago move between the goal pipes for the second game at Metropolitan Sports Center on April 6. This

Goalie Jim McLeod races behind the net while Real Lemieux of Los Angeles skates in pursuit. Barclay Plager keeps an eye on Lemieux and the puck.

time, the St. Louis shooters found the range and pumped five goals past the lean Minnesota goaltender, but it still wasn't sufficient. The North Stars also had scored five times, forcing the game into sudden-death overtime.

A minute-and-a-half had elapsed in the overtime when Jude Drouin of Minnesota shot hard at Blues goalie Ernie Wakely. Enroute the puck struck a stick and changed direction so abruptly that it struck Wakely in the face mask. Before the goaltender could recover, the puck fell at his skates, and Bill Goldsworthy of the home club pushed it into the net. Minnesota won the game 6–5 after one minute and thirty-six seconds of sudden death.

Philosophical coach Arbour pointed out that a lucky break often decides a sudden death win and he looked forward to bouncing back.

To some NHL critics, Arbour was whistling in the dark. The North Stars, they believed, were simply too strong for the new Blues. And new they were. So new, in fact, that Arbour decided to start 31-year-old goalie Jacques Caron, whose eleven-year career included only four NHL games before he joined St. Louis, and who, of course, had never before played in a Stanley Cup playoff.

"I knew if I waited long enough my time would come," said Caron. "I told my wife I'd make it to the NHL when I was 32, but I beat that by a year."

Caron had once seemed anything but a winner, but his performance was almost flawless. Fortunately, he received a little help from his friends, mostly from Phil "the Intimidator" Roberto, who had come to the Blues in mid-season. At 9:18 of the first period Mike Murphy forced Worsley into a deft save at the right side of the cage, but the rebound squirted to the left where "the Intimidator" smacked it home.

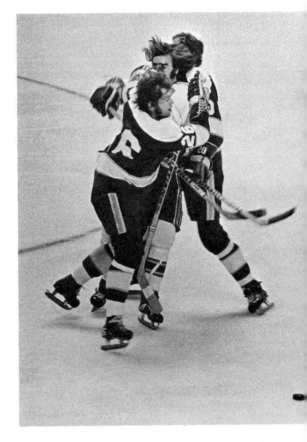

Irresistible force meets immovable object.

Jacques Caron, the concentrating goaltender.

Roberto Again

Roberto was the toast of the Arena again at 10:07 of the second period, scoring a power-play goal on a 20-foot screened shot. Jude Drouin made it close for Minnesota with a third period goal, but Caron held fast and the Blues won 2–1 reducing the North Stars' series lead to the same score.

Almost every observer agreed that the fourth game of the playoff on Sunday afternoon, April 9, would be decisive. A victory for the visiting North Stars would give them a 3–1 series lead, one that would be insurmountable. But if the Blues could somehow tie the play down, St. Louis had a chance to win the round.

Once again coach Arbour chose Caron to do the job for the Blues. Just how wise the decision was became a subject of debate both in and out of the locker room. After all, Caron had played just the night before and was visibly as well as audibly frazzled.

It's Bobby Orr and it means trouble.

"I didn't get to sleep until 3:30 or 4 A.M. after the Saturday night game," he said, "and I was up at 6:30 in the morning."

Before game time, Caron vomited his breakfast. "It was," he said in a rare understatement, "rough!"

But not nearly as rough as *he* was on the frustrated North Stars. Although Minnesota jumped into a 2–0 lead, jangled Jacques played superbly in goal and in the second period Roberto and Kevin O'Shea tied the score. Back and forth the clubs battled without a decisive score until the middle of the third period, when Dennis O'Brien and Moose Dupont were sent off with penalties.

An Abbreviated Power Play

Then Dennis Hextall of Minnesota was given two minutes for interference, enabling the Blues to ice four skaters to three for the North Stars. Enjoying an abbreviated power play, St. Louis crowded into the enemy end of the rink. The puck skimmed to Barclay Plager at the point, and he sent it right back to the net.

"It was supposed to have been a pass for Phil Roberto," Plager explained. "I saw him in front of the net with his stick up, and I tried to get the puck to him. He was in a good spot to deflect it. I think Maniago wanted to use his stick to keep Phil away, and then the puck hit him and went between his legs."

That made the score 3–2 for St. Louis, and that's how it ended. The series was tied at 2–2, and the experts were revising their assessment of the rejuvenated Blues. One obvious conclusion was that 23-year-old Phil "the Intimidator" had emerged as an authentic star.

"He's given us a lot of trouble," North Stars coach Jack Gordon allowed. "He had a chip on his shoulder in the first two games, running around the ice trying to stir up trouble. But in St. Louis he stuck to hockey and hurt us."

Whether the Minnesota strategists realized it or not, there was a method to Roberto's roughness. He had been assigned to shackle Bill Goldsworthy, the North Stars power shooter.

"Phil likes to rap people," said Garry Unger. "He's got some of their guys thinking more about what he's going to do to them than what they should be doing themselves."

Back to Minnesota

The series moved back to Minnesota for the fifth game on April 11. Despite the Blues' momentum home ice prevailed, although St. Louis managed to keep the game tied until the third period, when Drouin beat Caron to give the North Stars a 4–3 win.

As they prepared for the sixth game, the Blues realized they had to contain crafty Drouin if they were going to survive in the playoff.

Rugged Bob Plager had the answer. "Drouin doesn't like the rough stuff, so I'm going to work on him."

Plager did work over the North Stars, but it was the job he did on goalie Worsley that proved more decisive. With the score 2–1 for the Blues, Plager led a charge at the North Stars net. By the time the charge was completed, Worsley was lying unconscious in the goal crease, useless for the rest of the series.

Maniago took over as Gump's replacement and gave up a goal to Unger in the second period. Parise cut the

Bob Plager has a slight dispute.

69

Barclay Plager, ready for action.

margin at 15:01 of the third period, but Smoky Egers counterattacked for St. Louis and scored 72 seconds later. St. Louis won the game 4–2, and now the series was tied at three games apiece.

"I still think Minnesota has a chance," said a generous Bob Plager, "but this team has surprised even me. We're in it to win."

Nine and One-Half Million Spectators

The final game of the series was played on Sunday afternoon, April 16th, at Metropolitan Sports Center, before a nationally televised network audience numbering 9½ million. What they saw was one of the most exciting hockey games ever played.

All signs favored the North Stars. They had not lost any of the three previous home games, and they would be playing before a crowd of partisan fans. The Minnesotans were a playoff-hardened bunch of veterans, whereas the Blues were considerably less experienced.

"We have kids who never played in a Stanley Cup series before," said Arbour. "I think they've settled down, although they were nervous at first. We're confident we can win."

This confidence was translated into a goal at 12:04 of the first period, when Gary Sabourin deflected Bob Plager's shot from the point.

"Usually," said Plager wryly, "my shots travel so slowly that when the guys try to deflect them they stop them instead."

But the game was far from over. Maniago, who once again replaced Worsley, played superbly after Sabourin's score, but the North Stars simply couldn't beat Caron. At least, not until the opening minute of the third period. Almost magically, Charlie Burns of Minnesota drifted behind the St. Louis defense, took a pass from defenseman Ted Harris and backhanded the puck between Caron's legs.

"At that point," said J. P. Parise of Minnesota, "I thought we had them."

By all counts, the Blues were on the ropes. The North Stars had momentum and motivation but St. Louis had

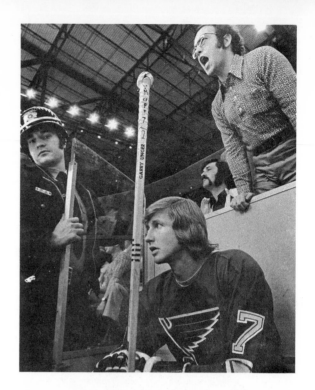

Two minutes for high-sticking!

Caron, and that was all they needed. Even when Murray Oliver of the North Stars split the Blues defense with 32 seconds remaining in regulation time, Caron was equal to the task.

Only history favored St. Louis. In 1968 the Blues and North Stars played a sudden-death match in the seventh and deciding game and St. Louis won it. Interestingly, Maniago was also the North Stars goalie on that occasion.

This time it appeared that Minnesota would exact revenge. Time after time the North Stars poured into the Blues' zone accompanied by wave upon wave of thunderous cheers from the home crowd, but they simply couldn't put the puck past Caron.

The Blues Erupt

Then the Blues erupted. Terry Crisp, one of the original 1967 Blues, skimmed a pass to Danny O'Shea, a former North Star. Danny spotted his brother, Kevin, speeding along the right wing and directed a lead pass to him. A Buffalo Sabres' reject, Kevin had been picked up on waivers by St. Louis for $30,000 only a month earlier. He was not renowned as a potent scorer, but this time, his shot was mighty.

It was delivered just as he sped over the Minnesota blue line, and it moved high and and hard at Maniago.

"I didn't think it was going in," said Kevin. "I thought it might have been a little high."

The puck streaked past Maniago at 10:07 of the sudden-death overtime, and as it did so the goalie peered hopefully over his right shoulder as the rubber struck the left upright with a resounding clang that could be heard throughout the arena. For an agonizing second the shot was *not* a goal.

"The puck hit the post behind me," said Maniago.

But the velocity of the shot carried the puck forward this time, *away* from the crease where Maniago desperately tried to right himself and control the rebounding disk. But there was no time.

"Before I could do anything," said Maniago, "the puck bounced off the top of my stick and fell into the

72

net. For a moment I must have been the only person in the building who knew it was in. There was a pause before the light went on, but the puck was too far back for me to reach it."

At first Kevin O'Shea didn't realize he had scored. "I heard the puck hit the post," he remembered, "and I was looking for the rebound. Then I saw my brother Danny with his stick in the air, and he was screaming, 'You scored! You scored!' It was unbelievable."

And so it was. Another beautiful chapter written in the short but thrilling life of the St. Louis Blues, marred only by the unkindly Boston Bruins, who beat the Blues in four straight games enroute to the 1972 Stanley Cup.

The conclusion of the Blues-Bruins playoff series, 1972.

the plager brothers

bob

*The many faces, moods and mayhem of
Bob Plager.*

barclay

There are competitors and there are competitors. But there is only one Barclay Plager!

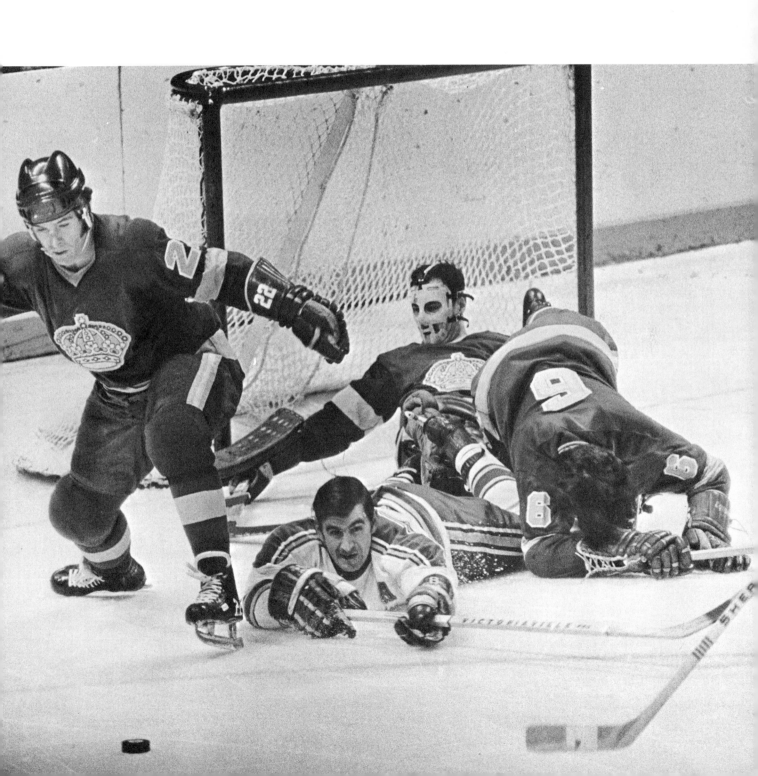

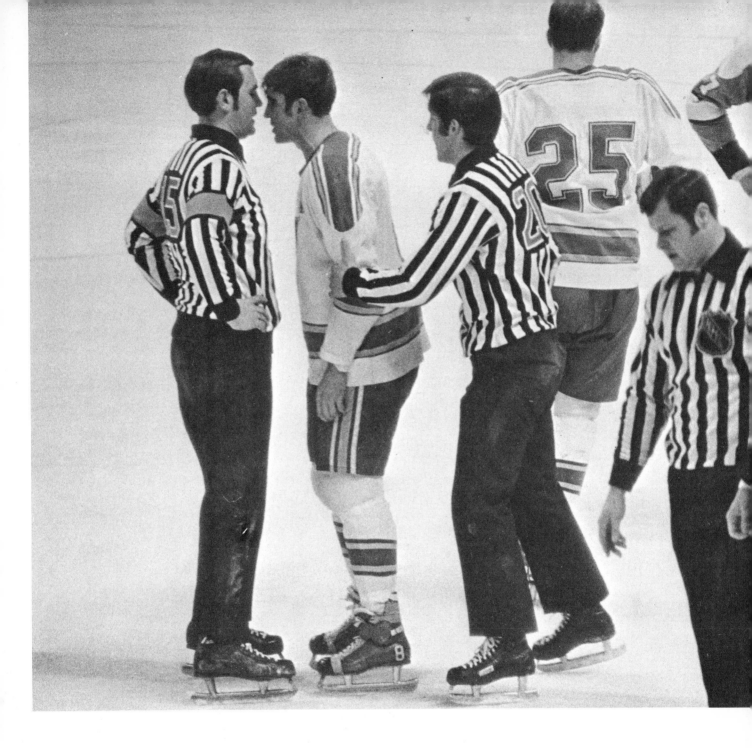

The many moves, moods and masks of
Jacques Caron.

goalkeeper caron

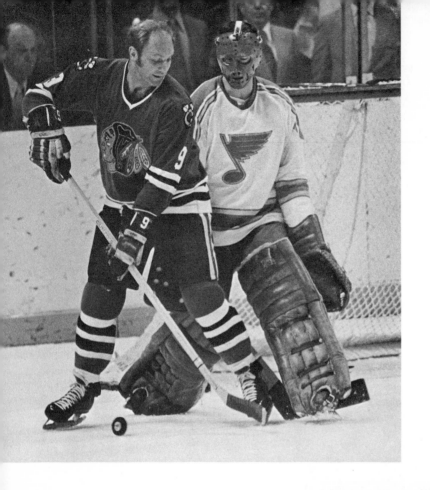

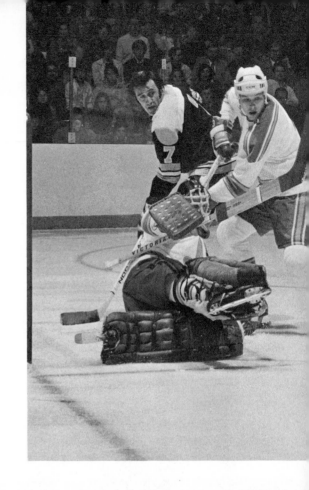

Jacques Caron sprawls for a spectacular save.

Johnny Bucyk (9) shoots for Boston but Jacques Caron makes the save.

Jacques Caron guards the goal.

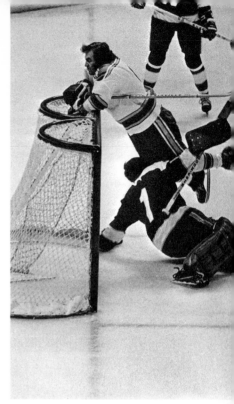

Collision Course! Robust Bob Plager misses his shot on goalie Gump Worsley of Minnesota during the 1972 Stanley Cup playoffs . . . Plager's brakes fail and he crashes headlong into the North Stars maskless netminder, knocking him unconscious.

garry unger

The galvanic Garry Unger.

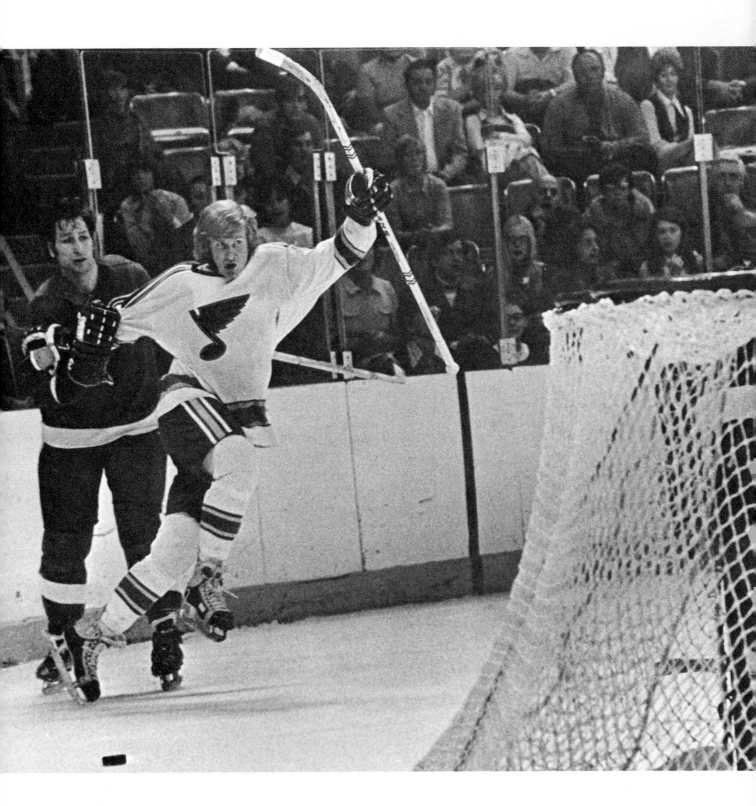

Garry Unger in action, at ease and in the locker room.

Boston Bruins goalkeeper Gerry Cheevers reaches the puck ahead of Mike Murphy and Garry Unger (7).

The Canuck is forelorn. The Blues are not.

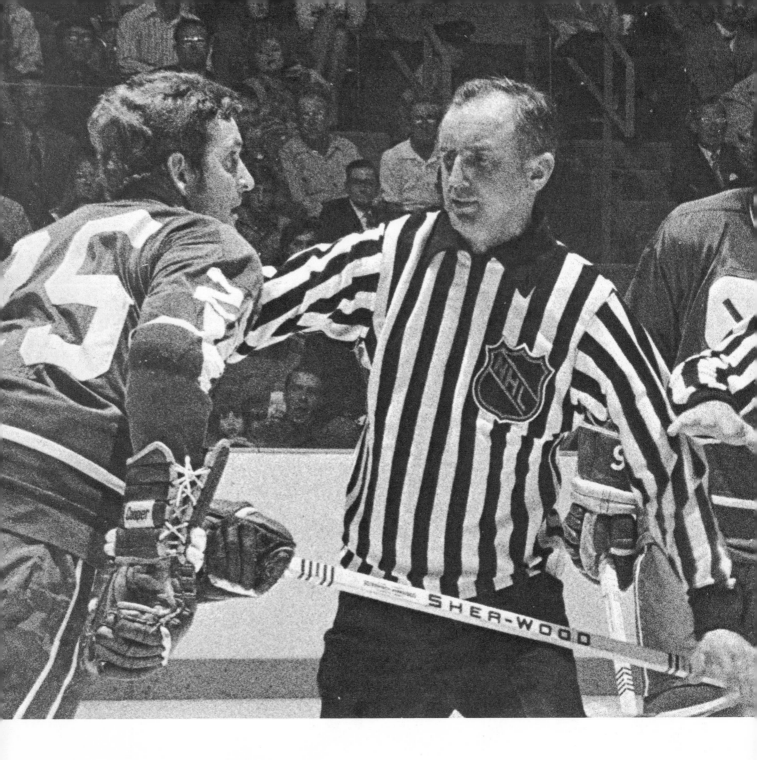

conflict

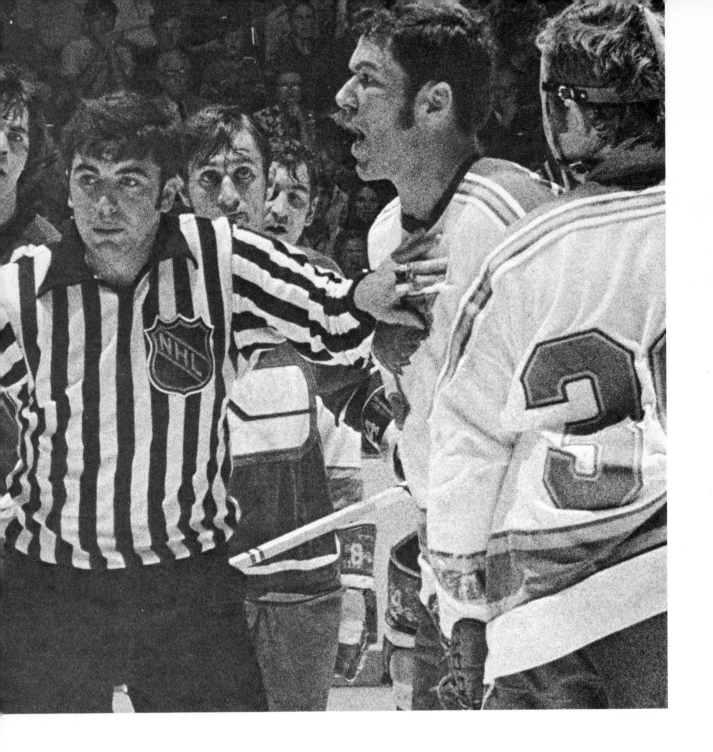

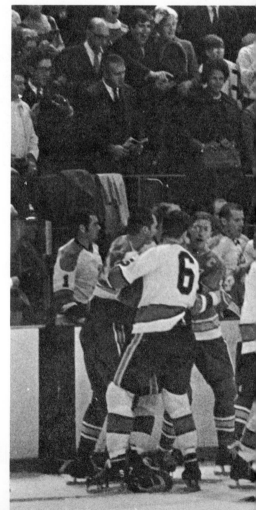

Mayhem on ice. Blues vs. Penguins with referee Art Skov studying the brawl from the ice.

Danny O'Shea lifts his stick in an attempt to screen the Toronto Maple Leafs' goalie, Bernie Parent.

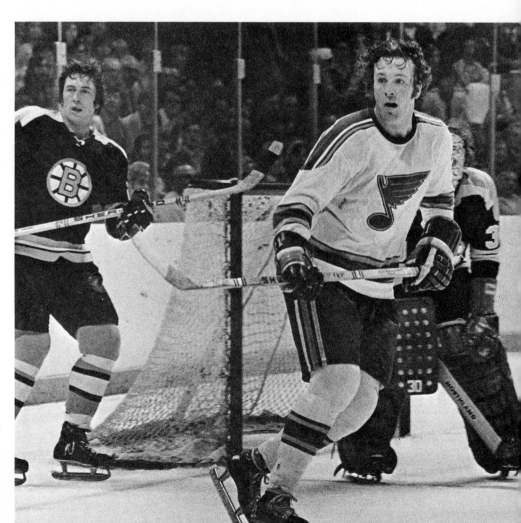

The smooth style of Kevin O'Shea.

Rare is the season when a brother act can make it to the NHL. It's even more un- usual when a big-league team can boast a pair of brother acts. Yet, the Blues did just that, first with the Plagers and then with the dynamic and productive O'Sheas— Danny and Kevin.

Kevin O'Shea appears unconcerned as Minnesota defenseman Ted Harris leans hard on his right elbow.

Phil Roberto against the Canucks . . .

and Bruins . . .

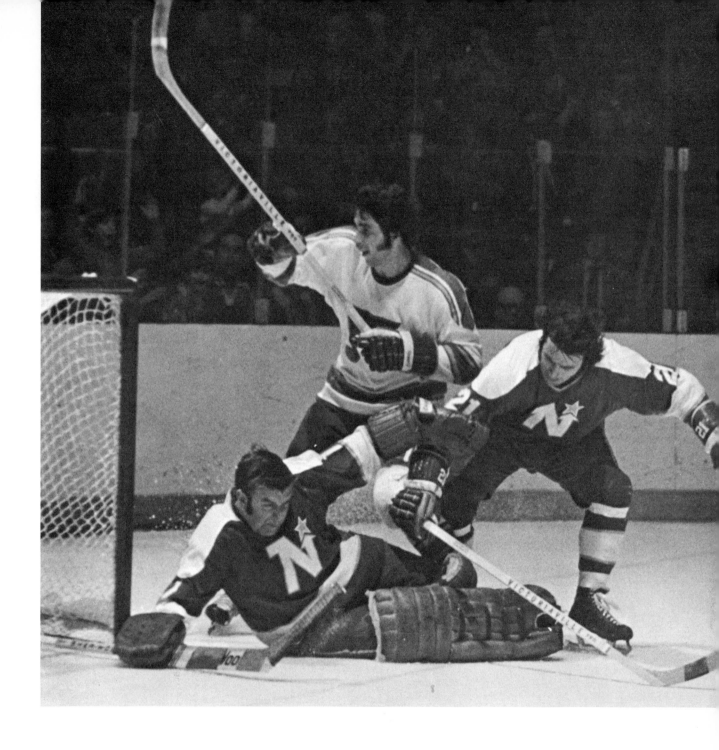

and North Stars . . .

The center of attraction—Phil Roberto.

and Rangers.

happiness is a thing called goal

Even Bobby Orr (4) couldn't stop Mike Murphy (l) Garry Unger and Jack Egers.

Boston defenseman Carol Vadnais wears dejected look for good reason. Terry Cris (12) has just scored.

Flyers' goalie Doug Favell appears mum-mified by Jack Egers (15) goal. Barclay Plager hails it from a distance.

"smokey" egers

Jack "Smokey" Egers, one of the hardest shots and toughest hombres in the National Hockey League.

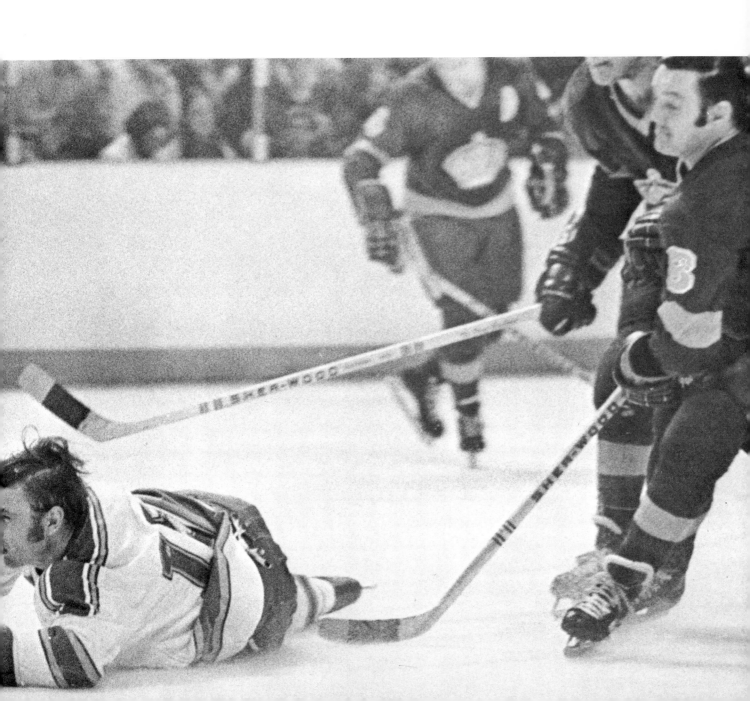

Frank St. Marseille tries to jar puck loose from Flyers' goalie Doug Favell.

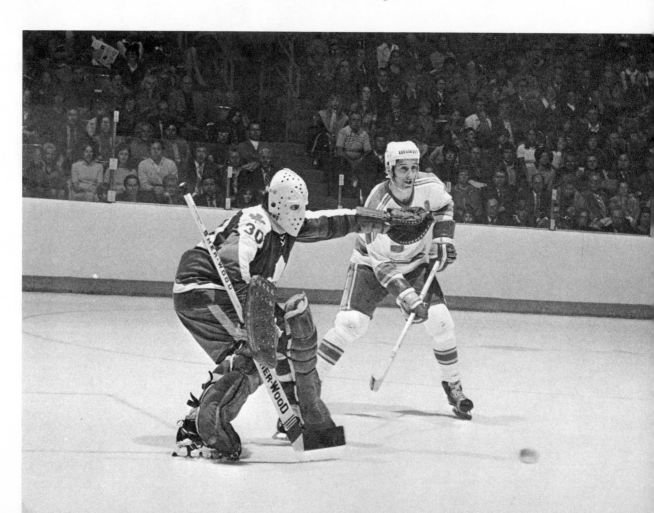

Frank St. Marseille laterals a pass in front of the Maple Leafs crease.

The bench. Gary Sabourin sitting, Jack
Egers standing.

Despite the Buffalo shuffle, Gary Sabourin
splits the defense.

Garry Unger skims a pass to Gary Sabourin against the Penguins.

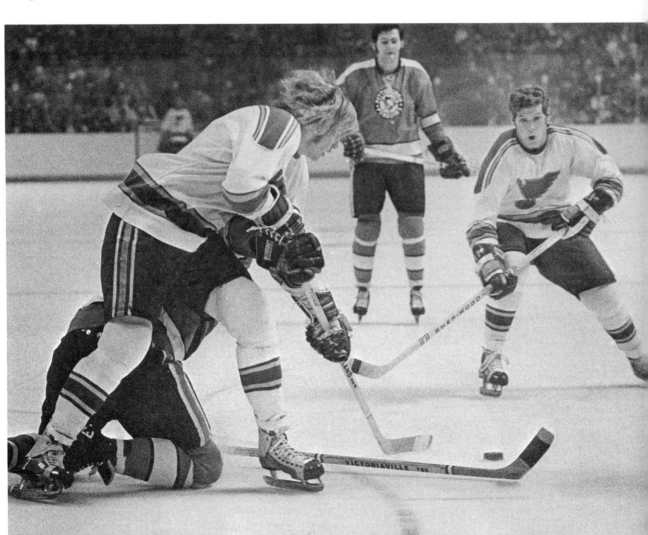

Andre "Moose" Dupont without helmet . . .

Once a Canadiens' farmhand, Andre Dupont battles his Montreal pals.

. . . and with helmet.

You're not going anywhere, fella!

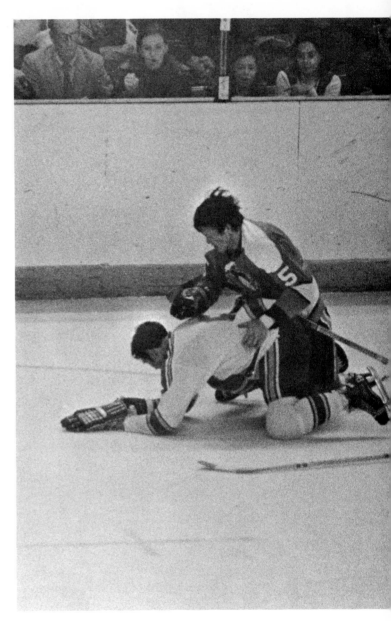

The scoring of a goal: Gary Sabourin eludes Chicago defenseman Bill White and moves in on goalie Tony Esposito who has sprawled in an attempted save . . . Sabourin pushes the puck under Esposito's upraised right pad . . . and into the twine!

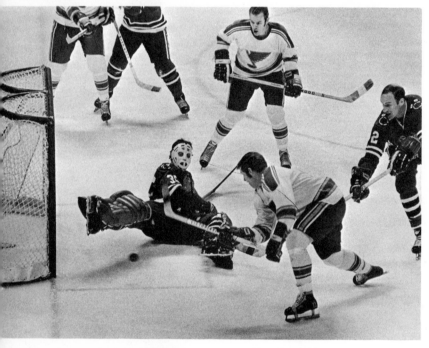

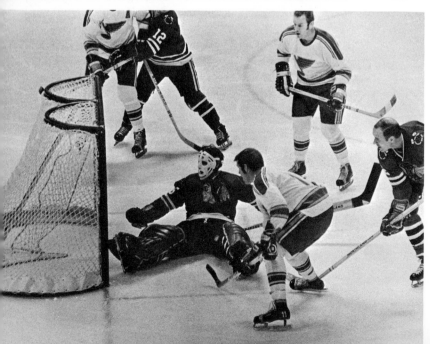

Just a little bit too high for Garry Unger.

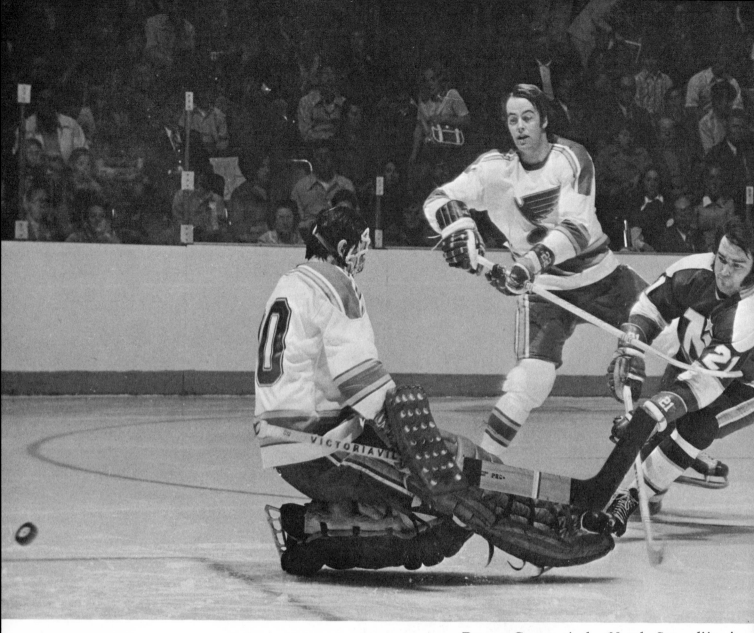

Danny Grant of the North Stars lifts it up—and in!

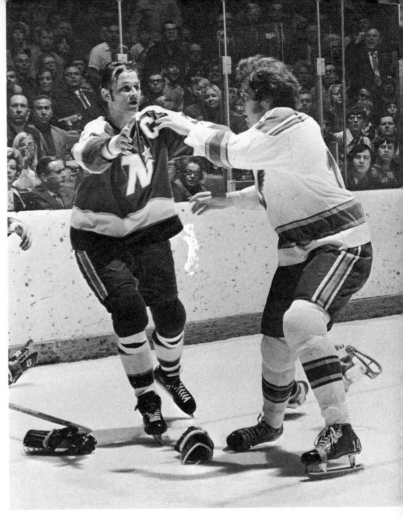

The defenseman and the goalie. Barclay
Plager and Jacques Caron.

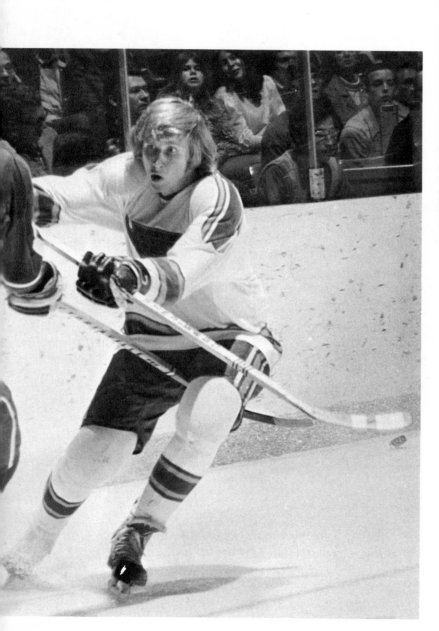